Deserts

KINGFISHER

Published in 2012 by Kingfisher
an imprint of Macmillan Children's Books
a division of Macmillan Publishers Limited
20 New Wharf Road, London N1 9RR
Basingstoke and Oxford
Associated companies throughout the world
www.panmacmillan.com

ISBN 978-0-7534-3422-2

First published as *Kingfisher Young Knowledge: Deserts* in 2005
Additional material produced for Macmillan Children's Books by Discovery Books Ltd

1 3 5 7 9 8 6 4 2
1TR/0512/UTD/WKT/140MA

A CIP catalogue record for this book is available from the British Library.

Printed in China

Note to readers: the website addresses listed in this book are correct at the time of going to print.
However, due to the ever-changing nature of the internet, website addresses and content can
change. Websites can contain links that are unsuitable for children. The publisher cannot be held
responsible for changes in website addresses or content, or for information obtained through
a third party. We strongly advise that internet searches be supervised by an adult.

Acknowledgements
The publisher would like to thank the following for permission to reproduce their material. Every care has been taken
to trace copyright holders. However, if there have been unintentional omissions or failure to trace copyright holders,
we apologise and will, if informed, endeavour to make corrections in any future edition.
b = bottom, *c* = centre, *l* = left, *t* = top, *r* = right

Photographs: *cover:* all images courtesy of Shutterstock.com; page 1: Getty Imagebank; 2–3 Corbis/Firefly Productions; 4–5
Corbis/Gavriel Jecan; 6–7 Getty Taxi; 8*t* Panoramic Images/Warren Marr; 8*b* Corbis/Dean Conger; 9*t* Corbis/Michael &
Patricia Fogden; 9*b* Corbis/Owen Franken; 10–11 Still Pictures/Frans Lemmens; 11*t* Corbis/Peter Johnson; 11*b* Corbis/Peter
Johnson; 12–13 Corbis/Peter Lillie; Gallo Images; 12*t* Panoramic Images/Warren Marr; 12*b* Science Photo Library/David
Scharf; 14–15 Getty Taxi; 14*b* Getty Imagebank; 15*tr* Corbis/Dewitt Jones; 15*br* Corbis/Martin Harvey; Gallo Images;
16–17 Getty National Geographic; 16*cr* Getty Imagebank; 16*b* NHPA/Darryl Balfour; 17*cl* NHPA/Martin Harvey; 17*r* Corbis;
18–19 Ardea/John Cancalosi; 18 Ardea/Pat Morris; 19 Minden Pictures ; 20–21 Corbis; 20*cl* Minden Pictures; 20*b* Frank Lane
Picture Agency; 21*tr* Michael & Patricia Fogden; 21*br* NHPA/Daniel Heuclin; 22–23 Getty Imagebank; 22*cr* Corbis/Martin
Harvey; Gallo Images; 23*tr* Ardea/Ken Lucas; 24–25 Getty Photographer's Choice; 25*tr* Corbis/Hans Georg Roth; 26–27 Still
Pictures; 27*tr* Corbis/Richard Powers; 28–29 Still Pictures; 29*tr* Corbis/Derek Trask; 30–31 Still Pictures; 30*b* Corbis/Janet
Jarman; 31*tr* Science Photo Library/Peter Ryan; 32–33 Corbis/KM Westermann; 32*bl* Getty Imagebank; 33*br* Getty
Imagebank; 34–35 Getty Stone; 34*cl* Corbis; 35*t* Corbis/Carl & Ann Purcell; 35*c* Corbis/Paul A Souders; 36–37 Corbis/Sergio
Pitamitz; 36*b* Getty Stone; 37*br* Corbis/Hughes Martin; 38–39 Science Photo Library/Martin Bond; 38*b* British Museum;
39*t* Getty National Geographic; 39*b* Corbis/James L Amos; 40–41 Alamy/Steve Bloom; 41*t* Getty National Geographic;
48*l* Shutterstock/Styve Reineck; 48*r* Shutterstock/Curioso; 49 Shutterstock/Patrick Poendi; 52*t* Shutterstock/Hagit Berkovich;
52*b* Joao Virissimo; 53 Shutterstock/James M Phelps, Jr; 56 Shutterstock/Songquan Deng

Commissioned artwork on page 7 by Encompass Graphics
Commissioned photography on pages 42–47 by Andy Crawford
Thank you to models Lewis Manu and Rebecca Roper

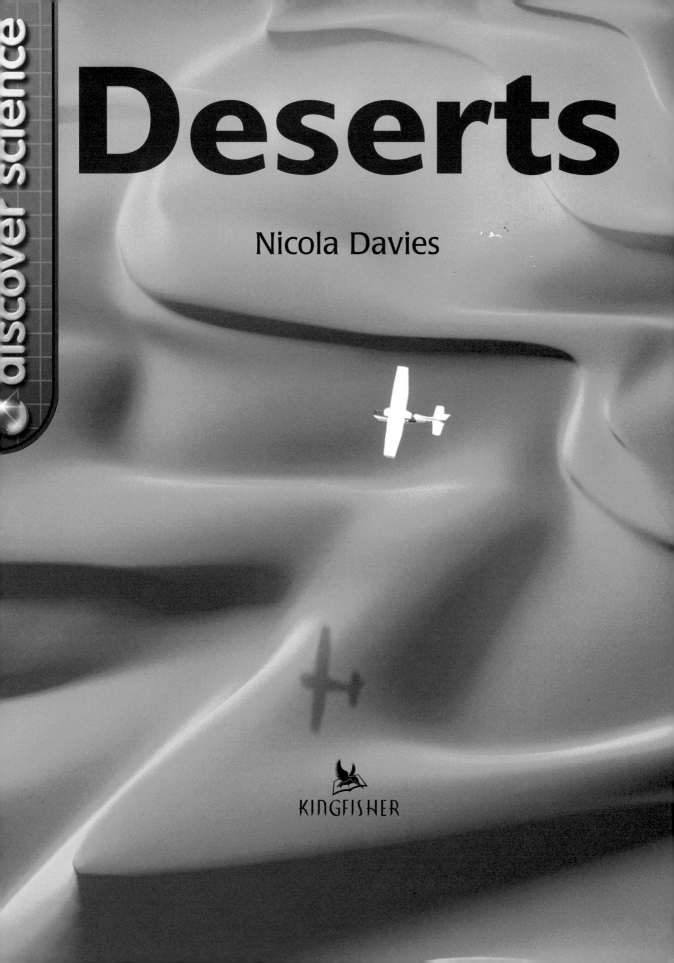

discover science

Deserts

Nicola Davies

KINGFISHER

Contents

What is a desert?

A desert is a place where it almost never rains. This makes these areas the driest places on Earth and the hardest to live in.

All around the world

Nearly a quarter of the land on our planet is covered in desert. Wherever there is desert, there are animals and plants that have found a way to survive the harsh, dry conditions.

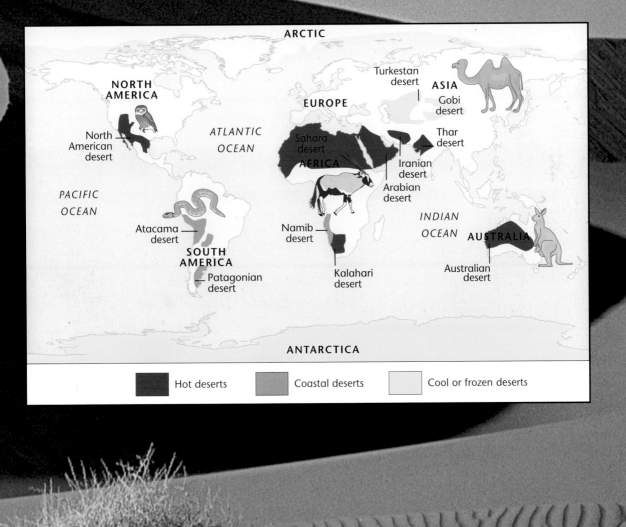

ARCTIC

NORTH AMERICA

North American desert

ATLANTIC OCEAN

EUROPE

Turkestan desert

ASIA

Gobi desert

Thar desert

Sahara desert

AFRICA

Iranian desert

Arabian desert

PACIFIC OCEAN

Atacama desert

SOUTH AMERICA

Namib desert

INDIAN OCEAN

AUSTRALIA

Australian desert

Patagonian desert

Kalahari desert

ANTARCTICA

Hot deserts   Coastal deserts   Cool or frozen deserts

Looking different

Not all deserts are hot and sandy. They can be pebbly, cool, rocky, mountainous or even a mixture of these. Every desert is unique!

Hot Mojave

The Mojave in North America was once the bottom of a lake. Now, it is a huge plain covered in cracked, dried mud and pebbles.

Cool Gobi

In Mongolia's Gobi desert, the wind always blows from the same direction. This shapes the sand dunes and pushes them forwards.

Hot Sahara

These rocks are found in mountains that are part of the Sahara. They are so high that they are covered in frost in the winter.

Coastal desert

Fog blows in from the sea next to the Namib desert. This brings water to some of the highest sand dunes in the world.

Wild weather

Desert weather is extreme. Clear blue skies mean that deserts are almost always sunny and hot during the day. But at night, it is a very different story.

Chilly nights

With no clouds to keep in the day's warmth, nights in the desert are very cold. Desert people light fires to keep warm after dark.

Roasting days

It may be freezing at midnight, but by midday in the desert it is really hot. Animals, such as these springboks, have to shelter from the Sun.

Keeping warm... and cool

Desert squirrels use their bushy tail to help them cope with the extremes of weather. In the cold night, the tail is like a fluffy blanket. But, during the hot day, it is a perfect sunshade.

Whistling wind

Deserts are so windy that almost every one has a wind with its own special name. For example, the wind in Algeria is called the Khamsin, and in North America it is called the Chubaseos.

Dusty gusts!

Sometimes, desert winds pick up sand and dust, and blow them around in storms that can last for days. This makes it hard to see and even to breathe.

Sandy sculpture

Gusts full of sand and dust slowly wear away rocks. Over thousands of years, the rocks are transformed into strange shapes, such as these amazing formations found in the Mojave desert.

Smoothest sands

Desert winds rub the sand grains together. This makes the grains smooth and round.

Desert rain

Rain in the desert is very rare. So, when there are showers, desert plants and animals have to make the most of them.

Stormy weather

Heavy rain often follows thunder and lightning. In some deserts, storms bring rain every year, but other deserts can stay dry for more than ten years.

Be quick!

As soon as it rains, frogs lay their eggs in the rainwater pools. Their tadpoles must grow quickly and change into frogs before the pools dry out.

Beautiful blooms

Desert plants flower after the rain, so the whole desert looks like a carpet of blossoms. When the flowers dry out and die, they leave seeds behind. These seeds sprout the next time it rains.

Prickly **plants**

Desert plants are tough. They have thicker skins, smaller leaves and more spines than other plants. This stops the heat from drying them out, and keeps hungry mouths away.

Drop that leaf!

Creosote bushes from North America drop their leaves when it is dry — but, when it rains, they grow them again.

The Namib's dew collector

Leaves of the strange-looking welwitschia plant bend over onto the ground. Fog and dew stick to the leaves, making droplets of water that run down to the roots.

Lots of spikes

Saguaro cacti from Arizona have no leaves. Instead, they store water in their huge stems. These stems are protected by thick skin and lots of prickly spikes.

Hide and seek!

Only the tops of the stone plant's two fat leaves peek above the ground's surface. The plant hides from the Sun and drying winds until it rains. Only then is it able to flower.

Desert fliers

Flight makes desert life easier for birds because they can travel long distances to find food and water. But they still have to cope with the hot days and cold nights.

Burrow nester

The tiny elf owl makes use of the cool twilight to hunt for small mammals, reptiles and insects. It nests underground, where its eggs are protected from the fierce heat that could easily cook them in their shells.

Cacti surgeons

Woodpeckers make holes in the rotten or broken stems of giant saguaro cacti. The woodpeckers nest in the cool holes and peck away any sick parts of the cactus. This stops disease from spreading to the whole plant.

Roadrunner stretches

Desert roadrunners warm up after the cold desert night by lifting their neck feathers and letting the Sun shine on a patch of special skin. This skin soaks up heat and keeps them warm.

Little creatures

Insects, reptiles and rodents thrive in the desert because they do not need much water. They can also hide from the heat, wind or cold in burrows.

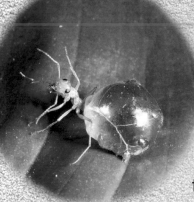

Honey tummies

Desert honey ants store precious water and nectar in their blown-up tummies. This store helps the ant colony to survive when there is no food or water.

Sleep by night

Reptiles such as this chuckwalla stay underground in the cold of night. When morning comes, they lie in the Sun to warm up.

Fog bathers

Darkling beetles find something to drink by trapping the droplets of water from fog on their legs, and tipping them towards their mouth.

Sleep by day

Animals such as this little gerbil are warm-blooded. They search for food in the cold night, but in the day they hide underground in burrows to keep cool.

Mighty mammals

Large mammals that live in deserts cannot shelter from the Sun in burrows like their smaller relatives do. They must find other ways to beat the heat.

Dig out to chill out

To cool their tummies, kangaroos scrape away at the hot surface sand and lie down on the colder sand underneath.

Colour-coded

Fennec foxes' pale fur
helps to reflect the heat
and to keep them cool – just
like a white T-shirt will keep
you cool on a hot summer's day.

Camel cooler

At night, camels' bodies become really
cold. So, although the Sun warms them
all day, they are never too hot.

Pools of water

Rivers flowing through the desert or bubbling up from under the ground can bring water all year round to deserts. A place where this happens is called an oasis.

Green and growing

Oases are bustling with life. Tall trees, such as palms, and many kinds of animals can live in oases because there is plenty of water.

Walking to water

Oases are very important to desert people and their animals. They may travel hundreds of kilometres to find water at a familiar oasis – even if the water is at the bottom of a well.

Desert dwellers

People have lived in deserts for thousands of years. They have learned all sorts of ways to cope with the difficulties of desert life.

People who wander

Many desert people are nomads. They live in tents and move about to find fresh water and grazing sites for their animals.

Water carriers

Women in India's
Thar desert carry
water from far-away
wells in large jars
that they balance
on their heads.

Growing deserts

Deserts are important and beautiful wild places. But they are expanding unnaturally because of some of the things that humans do. Every year, growing deserts swallow up valuable grassland, farmland and forest.

Too much munching

Where people let their animals eat all the plants, the Sun and wind can hit the bare ground. This turns the soil into dust and makes it difficult to regrow plants.

Bad gas!

Cars, aeroplanes and industry emit gases that make the weather hotter. This is called global warming. It is worse in places that are already hot and dry, so it makes deserts grow.

Making deserts green

People can help to stop deserts from expanding by planting trees and grass to protect the soil. Irrigating the desert helps to keep the plants alive.

Rain saving

Saving rainwater with dams means that there will be water for crops. This woman is harvesting food in what was once desert.

Magic water

Usually, water runs through sand and is lost. Adding flakes of special plastic to the water helps soil to hold on to it and the plants to grow.

Green... and greener

Growing plants also helps to cool the ground and the air above. This means that the soil stays moist and the desert cannot expand.

Cities in the desert

There are cities in deserts all over the world. But cities with millions of people use a lot of water – and that is a big problem in any desert!

Bright lights, big city
Las Vegas, in America's Nevada desert, is so big that it uses water from hundreds of kilometres away. This lack of water threatens both the wildlife and farmland with drought.

Green, green city

Abu Dhabi, on the coast of the United Arab Emirates, uses fresh water from the sea by taking out the salt! This means there is enough water to create green spaces that keep the city cool.

Ways to save water

Kerzaz, an ancient city in the Sahara, needs far less water than a modern town. People there use water carefully and know that every drop is very precious.

Using the desert

Deserts may look empty, but they have hidden treasures. They also give us the space to do things that are dangerous anywhere else.

Deadly testing

The world's deadliest weapons, nuclear bombs, were tested in deserts where they could not kill anyone. But these bombs left the land poisoned for many years after testing.

Hidden energy

Petroleum oil is found under some deserts. It is pumped and carried to cities and other countries in huge pipes like this one.

Underground jewels

Opals were formed
millions of years ago
when water drained
from rocks under
the ground. This
ground is now the
Australian desert
and almost all of
the world's opals
are mined there!

Lots of fun!

Sunny blue skies and beautiful scenery make deserts great places to relax, but some people prefer a bit more action.

Sandboarding

You can go down a sand dune in just the same way that you would slide down a snowy slope. You can even surf a dune like a big wave in the sea!

Desert racer

Sandbuggies can climb steep dunes and zoom about the desert without getting stuck in the sand. They are great fun but their tyres can damage desert plants.

Comfortable climbing

Rock formations found in deserts are warm and dry. This makes them easier to climb than mountains where the weather can be cold, wet and icy.

History in the desert

We can learn about the past in deserts because the hot, dry air preserves dead bodies. Sand covers the dried remains of people, plants and animals and, because few people live in the deserts, they can lie undisturbed for a long time.

Mummies from long ago

Bodies buried in deserts dry out very quickly, so skin, hair and clothes can last for thousands of years. Preserved dead bodies, called mummies, found in deserts show us how people looked and dressed a long time ago.

Rock art

Thousands
of years ago,
people painted
pictures on rocks in the
Namib. They show that the desert
used to be grassland bustling
with people and animals.

Desert dinos

Some of the world's most
exciting dinosaur fossils
have been found in deserts.
The dry winds wear away
the rock and bring fossil
bones close to the surface.

Ice and water

Not all deserts are hot and dusty – some are found in the coldest parts of the world! The word desert can also be used to describe places where conditions are simply too tough for life to survive.

Lifeless blue

There can be no life in the sea without phyto-plankton. In places where plankton does not grow, the sea can be a wet and salty desert.

Icy deserts

Some parts of the Arctic receive less rain than Africa's Sahara desert. These areas are too cold and dry for anything to grow. Polar bears survive by walking to the sea to catch seals.

Crazy camels

Salt train

Selling salt is a very important way for desert people to make money. Loads of salt are carried across the desert on camels.

camel template

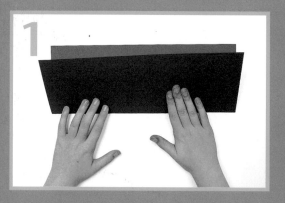

You will need
- Brown card
- Tracing paper
- Pencil
- Scissors
- Permanent marker
- Foil chocolate wrappers
- Glue
- Gold or silver thread

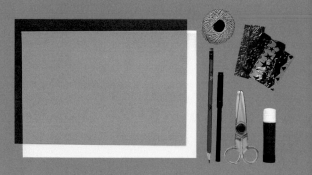

1

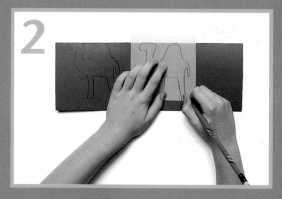

Fold the brown card in half. Put the piece of tracing paper over the camel template and trace over the camel shape.

2

Put the traced template onto the card so that the camel's hump is on the fold. Trace the camel onto the card to make three camels.

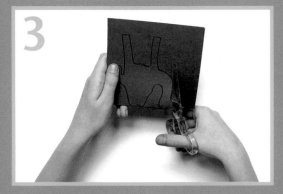

3

Using the scissors, carefully cut out the three camel shapes. Make sure that you do not cut through the humps at the fold.

4

Holding the camel firmly with one hand, use the permanent marker to draw the eyes and the noses on each camel.

5

Smooth out three different foil chocolate wrappers. Paste them over the middle of the camels' backs. You may need to cut the wrappers if they are too long.

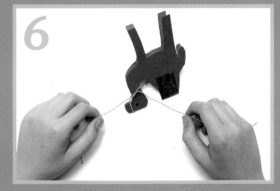

6

To make the camels' bridles, tie thread around the camels' necks. Use the thread to join the camels together so that they are ready to carry salt across the desert.

3-D cactus

Slit and slide!

The saguaro cactus can be over 10 metres tall and have five arms. Some saguaro are over 200 years old!

You will need
- Pencil
- Tracing paper
- Thick green card
- Scissors

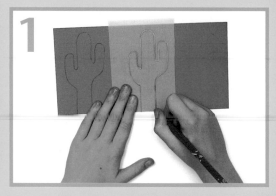

Trace the cactus template onto the tracing paper. Then, use the template to trace two cacti onto the green card.

Cut out the two cactus shapes. Following the template, use the scissors to cut a slit half-way down one cactus.

slit 1 (step 2)

cactus template

slit 2 (step 3)

Cut a slit half-way up the second cactus. Slide the first cactus into the second. If you like, decorate the cactus with green glitter.

Palm trees

You will need

- 2 strips of brown card
- Glue
- Green card
- Double-sided tape
- Shoebox lid
- Sand

Bend and shape it!

Palm trees are often found at oases in the Sahara. Desert people rest in the shade of the palms when it is hot.

To make the palm's trunk, glue the brown card to make an 'L' shape. Fold the card over itself to make a concertinaed tube.

To make the palm's leaves, cut the green card into five curved strips. Fold each strip like a fan and it will spring open.

Fill a shoebox lid with sand and put the camels, 3-D cactus and palm tree in the tray to create your own desert landscape.

Cut a small piece of double-sided tape and stick it in the middle of the palm's trunk. Stick each of the five leaves onto the trunk.

Aboriginal spinning top

Clever symbols
The Aboriginal people of Australia's desert painted symbols on rocks. Now, artists use these symbols to paint modern art.

You will need
- Pencil
- Mug
- Cup
- Side plate
- Card
- Scissors
- Paint
- Paintbrush
- Modelling clay
- Compass
- Chopstick

emu

campfire

child

1

To make five disks, draw on the card around a mug two times, a cup two times and a side plate once. Carefully cut out each disk.

2

Paint the disks using orange or yellow paint – if you like, each circle can be a different colour. Leave the disks to dry thoroughly.

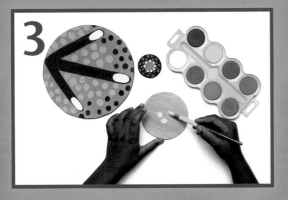

Following the examples on page 46, paint one side of each disk with a different Aboriginal symbol. When the paint is dry, turn the disks over and paint the same symbol on the other side.

Put a ball of modelling clay under the middle of each disk. Use the point of the compass to pierce a hole in the middle of each disk.

When all five disks are on the chopstick, stand the top upright and spin it around.

To put the disks on the chopstick, start with one of the disks from the cup and the mug, then the disk from the plate and the last two from the mug and cup. The disks should be evenly spaced.

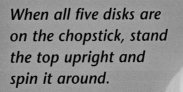

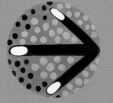

Glossary

Burrows – holes or tunnels under the ground

Bustling – busy

Conditions – how things are around you

Dew – small drops of water that form in the night on grass and plants

Drought – a long period of time when there is no water

Emit – to give off

Expanding – getting bigger

Extreme weather – very hot or cold, dry or wet, or very windy weather

Fog – a low cloud of tiny drops of water

Formations – patterns

Fossils – the remains of ancient animals or plants turned to rock

Global warming – an increase in the world's overall temperature, thought to be caused by pollution

Gusts – sudden blasts of wind

Irrigating – watering big areas, such as whole fields

Mammals – warm-blooded animals that feed their young on milk produced by the mother

Moist – damp

Nomads – people who move from place to place, taking their homes with them

Oasis – a place in the desert where there is water

Petroleum oil – the oil used to make fuel for vehicles, to generate electricity and to make many plastics

Phyto-plankton – the tiny floating plants found in oceans and seas

Plain – a huge flat area of land

Rare – when something does not happen very often

Reflect – to bounce back

Survive – to stay alive

Tadpoles – young frogs and toads

Transformed – changed

Twilight – when it is not dark or light, at dawn and at dusk

Warm-blooded – warm-blooded animals have bodies that can make their own heat

Well – a deep hole in the ground with water at the bottom

This book includes material that would be particularly useful in helping to teach children aged 7–11. It covers many elements of the English and Science curricula, and some cross-curricular lessons involving Geography and Art.

Extension activities

Writing
Write a report about how animals and plants have adapted to life in a desert (see pp11, 15, 16–17, 18–19, 20–21, 22–23). You could think about themes such as nests or reproduction.

Read pages 28–33. Write a short article persuading people to stop creating more deserts, and suggesting how we can change our behaviour.

Imagine you are a desert nomad (see pp10, 24–25, 26). Write a diary describing how you spend a week. Think about how nomads cope with life in the desert and how they might feel.

How would you survive in the desert? How would you stay cool in the day and keep warm at night? Where could you get water from and what could you eat? Write a short story where a character is stranded in the desert and is saved by finding an oasis.

Speaking and listening
Some people might be surprised that not all deserts are hot and sandy (see pp8–9 and 40–41). Make a short presentation explaining why parts of the Arctic and Antarctica can be deserts.

Science
The whole book links with the science topic of habitats. Other topics with links in this book include rocks and soils (pp8–9, 12–13, 35, 37, 38–39), animals and life cycles (pp11, 15, 16–17, 18–19, 20–21, 22–23, 24–25, 41) and plant life (pp15, 16–17, 19, 24–25, 31).

Page 39 tells you about desert fossils, but did you know sand contains old shells from dead sea animals? Try to find some by putting some natural sand in a bowl and adding vinegar. The old shell fragments will fizz. How many different types of shell can you see?

Cross-curricular links
Geography: There is material on the topics of weather (pp10–11, 14, 29) and the environment (pp28–29, 30–31, 32–33).

Look at the map on page 7. Which desert is nearest to where you live? Can you find it in an atlas and work out how far away it is?

Research the different ways people and animals find water in the desert. Create a poster or table to show what you have discovered.

Art: Create a collage showing different parts of the desert. You could show rock formations, sand dunes, an oasis and life underground.

Using the projects
Children can follow or adapt these projects at home. Here are some ideas for extending them:

Pages 42–43: Make a snake from an egg carton. Cut out the cups and carefully poke holes in them with a sharp pencil. Thread a piece of wool through one cup and tie a knot in the end, thread the other end through the other cups and tie them off to make a slithery snake.

Page 45: Try adding an oasis to your desert landscape. Some shiny card would look good as water.

Pages 46–47: Look at the large, swirly fossil on page 39. Create a fossil picture using potato prints or fingerprints.

Did you know?

- More than one billion people, one-sixth of the Earth's population, actually live in desert regions.

- When captured, the tiny elf owl will play dead until all danger has passed.

- Camels store fat in their humps, not water. Baby camels are born without a hump because the layer of fat doesn't develop until they eat solid food.

- A place that receives less than 25 centimetres of rain in a year is considered a desert.

- The Joshua tree is only found in the Mojave desert and relies solely on one kind of moth for pollination.

- The fennec fox's ears are 15 centimetres long. They help the fox to radiate body heat and to keep cool in the desert heat.

- Twenty per cent of the Earth's land surface is made up of desert.

- Desert tortoises spend more than 95 per cent of their lives in underground burrows. This is because the ground temperature outside can reach more than 60°C.

- The Tuareg people live in the Sahara and are sometimes known as the 'blue people' because of the colour of their traditional blue dress.

- Camels can last up to a week without water and then may drink up to 145 litres in one go.

- The Sahara desert is the second largest desert in the world after Antarctica, but it is the largest hot desert in the world.

- When full, a saguaro cactus stem can store up to five tonnes of water, which is enough for it to survive many months of drought.

- Roadrunners can reach speeds of up to 27 kilometres per hour. They are so fast that they can catch and eat rattlesnakes.

- Camels have hairy ears to stop sand entering them during sandstorms. They can also close their nostrils, and have two layers of eyelashes to help protect themselves when it is windy.

- Elf owls don't make any noise as they approach their prey. This is called 'silent flight'.

- The Mojave desert spans four American states – Arizona, California, Nevada and Utah.

Deserts quiz

The answers to these questions can all be found by looking back through the book. See how many you get right. You can check your answers on page 56.

1) Where does the elf owl make its nest?
   A – In a tree
   B – In a cactus
   C – Underground

2) How does the roadrunner warm up?
   A – It runs very fast
   B – It lifts the feathers on its neck for the Sun to heat up a special patch of skin
   C – It lies in the morning Sun

3) What does the saguaro cactus store in its stems?
   A – Water
   B – Nothing
   C – Ice

4) Where do darkling beetles find a drink?
   A – From the leaves of desert plants
   B – They trap water from dew on their legs and slide it into their mouths.
   C – From the surface of rocks

5) What do desert honey ants store in their tummies?
   A – Honey
   B – Water and nectar
   C – Water

6) What is the name given to people who live in the desert and move from place to place?
   A – Herders
   B – Shepherds
   C – Nomads

7) How do kangaroos keep cool?
   A – They go for a swim
   B – They hop into the shade
   C – They dig a hole in the hot sand and lie in the cool sand underneath

8) What is an area of water in the desert called?
   A – An oasis
   B – A river
   C – A puddle

9) Where does the city Abu Dhabi get its water from?
   A – From rain
   B – From the sea
   C – From wells deep underground

10) Where in the world are most opals mined?
   A – America
   B – Europe
   C – Australia

11) What is the name given to bodies that are preserved and found in the desert?
   A – Mummies
   B – Corpses
   C – Dummies

12) How are people trying to stop deserts expanding?
   A – By letting animals eat all the plants
   B – By planting new trees and plants and saving rainwater
   C – By increasing global warming

Find out more

Books to read

100 Questions and Answers: Desert Animals by Jen Green, Parragon Plus, 2000

Desperate Deserts (Horrible Geography) by Anita Ganeri, Scholastic, 2008

I Wonder Why the Sahara is Cold at Night? And Other Questions About Deserts by Jackie Gaff, Kingfisher, 2002

Life Cycles: Desert by Sean Callery, Kingfisher, 2012

Life in the Desert (What on Earth) by Gerald Legg, Book House, 2006

The Cat in the Hat Knows a Lot About That!: Why Oh Why are Deserts Dry? by Tish Rabe, Bantam Children, 2011

Places to visit

Drusillas Park Zoo, Alfriston, East Sussex
www.drusillas.co.uk
Visit this fun zoo and park for a great day out. You can see the rare fennec fox, explore the Eden's Eye adventure maze and go crazy in the Go Wild! adventure playground.

Eden Project, Cornwall
www.edenproject.com
Have a great day out at this amazing venue, which displays incredible plants that thrive during drought, stunning sculpture and amazing gardens. The *Core* education centre holds some hands-on exhibits about climate change, evolution and ecosystems. The moving *Plant Engine* exhibit explains all the amazing things that plants do for us.

ZSL Whipsnade Zoo, Bedfordshire
www.zsl.org/zsl-whipsnade-zoo
Visit this spectacular zoo and meet some of the most majestic desert animals alive, including Bactrian camels, meerkats and ostriches.

Websites

www.bbc.co.uk/schools/gcsebitesize/science/ edexcel/environment/evolutionrev2.shtml
Visit this educational website to find out how animals and plants have adapted to living in the desert. You can also watch a video to see how the saguaro cactus stores water in its stem.

http://environment.nationalgeographic.com/ environment/habitats/desert-profile/
Check out this website to find out all about deserts. You can also view photos of some of the desert's most well-adapted animals and see how global warming is affecting these habitats.

www.oxfam.org.uk/coolplanet/ontheline/ explore/nature/deserts/deserts.htm
Explore this website to find out about one of the Earth's most extreme environments – deserts. You can discover all about the climate, landscape, plant and animal life and much more.

Deserts quiz answers

1) C	7) C
2) B	8) A
3) A	9) B
4) B	10) C
5) B	11) A
6) C	12) B